WHAT'S THE MATTER WITH PLUTO?

The Story of Pluto's Adventures With the Planet Club

By Paul Halpern, Ph.D.

Illustrated by Vance Lehmkuhl

The Planet Club was an old and distinguished society.

Becoming a member of the group was very special.

THIS IS TO CERTIFY THAT

Jupiter

IS A MEMBER IN GOOD STANDING OF THE

PLANET CLUB

To join it, you couldn't be just any old object in space.
You needed to have just the right qualities.

A team of judges called astronomers made the
decision by examining each candidate very carefully.

Earth was a friendly planet full of life.
She proudly displayed her deep blue seas,
lush green forests, and puffy white clouds.
She was round, like the other planets,
and gracefully revolved along with them.

But she could remember a time,
hundreds of years ago,
before astronomers let her
into the Planet Club.

The reason Earth was originally left out had to do with the Planet Club's name.

"Planet" in Greek means "wanderer." Early astronomers in ancient Greece and elsewhere had noticed that the planets seem to wander through the sky instead of moving together like the groupings of stars called constellations.

For example, while the starry pattern that forms the constellation Orion (the Hunter) always travels together through the sky, planets meander on their own.

Gazing up instead of down, early astronomers overlooked Earth. They did not see it move through the sky, let alone wander. Instead, their first choices for the Planet Club were Mercury, Venus, Mars, Jupiter and Saturn. These were the only points of light astronomers could see that seemed to meander. It was before telescopes were invented, so astronomers made their selection using their eyes, not instruments.

Those five planets were very happy to be chosen. They were delighted to be watched and to know that astronomers were mapping out their movements. Whenever they would line up close together in the sky, in arrangements called conjunctions, they would pose and smile for the astronomers, pleased to be getting so much attention.

To display their talents, they would sometimes perform a little trick. While normally they would move one way across the sky, sometimes they would seem from astronomers' viewpoints to reverse their motions, moving backward. Then, after a while, they would appear to switch directions and move forward again.

Secretly, they knew the reason for the retrograde motion, as it was called, but they wanted to see if astronomers could figure it out.

One day, a very clever Polish astronomer named
Nicholas Copernicus deciphered the riddle.
He figured out that if the planets were moving
around the Sun, rather than around the Earth,
they would appear sometimes to travel backward
when they were actually going in the same direction.
The reason is that they would sometimes lag behind
Earth in their orbits. Copernicus's discovery meant
that Earth moves around the Sun too,
like the other planets.

In 1609, Italian astronomer Galileo Galilei was the first to aim a telescope at the sky. In doing so, he helped prove Copernicus's theory that Earth and the other planets behaved similarly in revolving around the Sun. By looking closely at the members of the Planet Club, he showed that many of them had features in common with Earth.

For example, he revealed that just as Earth's closest companion is the Moon, Jupiter had moons going around it too. Because of similarities between the members of the Planet Club and Earth it was clear that Earth should be a member too!

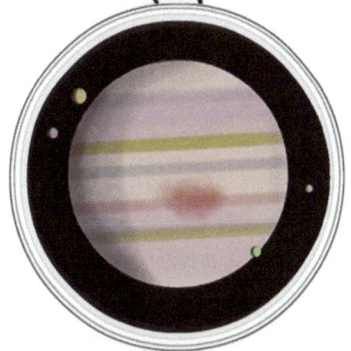

Due to Galileo's discoveries, matching up with
Copernicus's theory, the membership rules for
the Planet Club changed. All round objects
orbiting the Sun were invited to join,
including Earth.

Still, the Club excluded many other objects that
belonged to the Solar System. The rocky bodies
called asteroids and the icy bodies called comets
were not let in, because they were irregularly shaped.
Besides, they appeared smaller and often had more
stretched-out paths.

Also, because the moons circled the planets
instead of the Sun directly they were not
admitted to the Planet Club. The moons of
Jupiter didn't mind, as there were so many
of them that they tended to socialize together.
They also looked up to Jupiter, proud that
he was the largest planet.

Earth's Moon, on the other hand,
often confessed to being lonely.
She felt jealous that Earth was
part of a Club she couldn't join.

In the 18th and 19th centuries, thanks to British astronomers William Herschel and John Couch Adams, French mathematician Urbain Le Verrier, and German astronomer Johann Galle, the Club gained two important new members: Uranus and Neptune. Herschel discovered Uranus in 1781 when he was searching for stars using a telescope that was six inches in diameter.

At first he thought that he had found a new star, but when he mapped out its motion he found that it orbited the Sun much farther away than Saturn. Uranus was thrilled to be noticed and overjoyed to be granted full membership in the Planet Club!

Neptune's admission was a two-step process. The first step was when Le Verrier and Adams each noticed that something unseen was tugging on Uranus making its orbit have a slight wobble. Each estimated that another planet, farther away than Uranus, was causing the pulling through the invisible force of gravity. It turned out to be Neptune just trying to get astronomers attention.

Galle looked with his telescope in the part of the sky predicted by Le Verrier and found a happy Neptune smiling back at him.

The Planet Club members had many fun times together, especially once there were eight of them. Although they all got along well with each other, when they played together they naturally formed two teams.

One team, including Jupiter, Saturn, Uranus, and Neptune, were the gas giants. These were much larger and colder than the other planets and lived in the outer part of the Solar System. Rather than having solid surfaces, they were made of mixtures of gases such as hydrogen and helium. Of these, Neptune was the farthest away from the Sun.

With their whopping sizes, each of the gas giants
attracted many moons. Not just Jupiter, but also
Saturn, Uranus and Neptune each had large groups.
Impressed with their girth, the moons
circled around them like loyal fans.

Each of the
gas giants
also had rings.

Saturn was
especially
proud of
her stunning
collection.
They were
formed of the finest
pieces of ice,
arranged in many
circles around her,
gleaming in sunlight.
The rings of the other
gas giants were not as
noticeable as Saturn's,
but could still be observed
by astronomers.

The other team in the Planet Club, consisting
of Mercury, Venus, Earth, and Mars, were the
rocky planets. These were relatively small and
had solid surfaces.

None of them had rings
and only two of them had moons:
Earth's Moon and Mars's
little moons Phobos and Deimos.

Of these rocky planets,
Mercury was the tiniest
and closest to the Sun.

Mercury and Neptune,
the innermost and
outermost planets,
liked to tease each other
playfully about their differences.
Mercury joked about Neptune's
slow pace as she crept along
her orbit like a tortoise.
While it took Mercury only 88 days
to orbit the Sun, it took Neptune
165 years. In fact, Neptune
has completed only one orbit
since the planet's discovery!

"Been around the Sun recently?"
Mercury often said to Neptune.

Neptune's ready comeback was to tease
Mercury for being a lightweight.

"Lift anything heavy recently?"
Neptune replied.

"Such as gases?"
said Mercury. "Big deal!"

"Ices too!" said Neptune. "Ices and gases
are pretty bulky when there are
so much of them!"

"I see why you move so slow!
You are really carrying a lot!"
said Mercury.

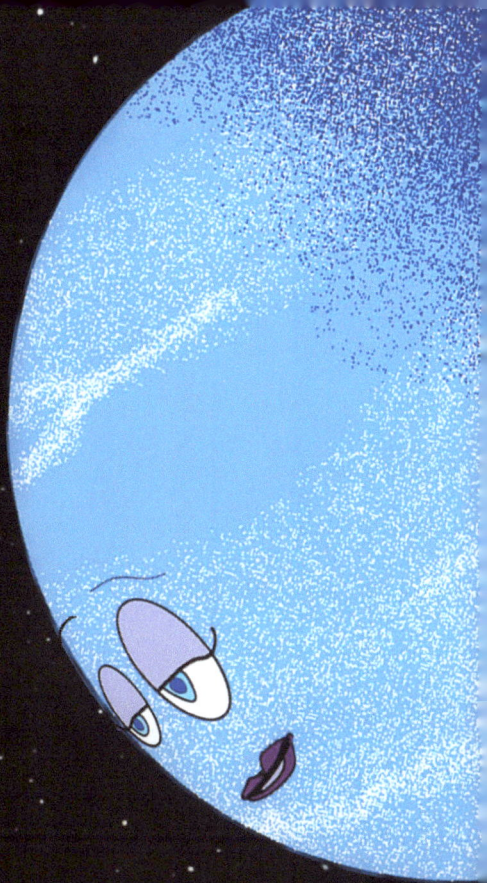

"Well, actually my orbit
takes so long because I am
so far away from the Sun.
Thanks for trying to
understand my point of view.
We outer planets cannot
revolve as quickly as you!"
said Neptune, appreciating
Mercury's sympathy.

The early 20th century brought one new addition to the Planet Club. In the winter of 1930, American astronomer Clyde Tombaugh was scanning the skies above Arizona hoping to find a possible new planet that was predicted to be beyond Neptune.

Night after freezing cold night, he took photographs of the stars. He compared the pictures to each other, hoping to see something that had wandered from night to night.

Finally, in February of that year, he found the planet he had sought.

Astronomers debated what to call the new planet.
An eleven-year-old English girl named Venetia Burney
came up with the winning suggestion.
While sitting at the breakfast table with her grandfather,
she heard about the discovery. She had studied
the Roman gods, and knew that Pluto was the god
of the underworld, where it is cold and dark.

Because the new planet was so far away,
she realized that it would be cold and dark too.
So she said to her grandfather, "Why not call it
Pluto?" Her grandfather contacted an astronomer,
who passed along the suggested name to others,
and they approved it.

Pluto liked his name very much. He was delighted that a child named him. "'Planet Pluto' has a nice sound to it," he thought. "Plus, it is plenty pleasing." He continued to try to think of "pl" words as he slowly orbited.

Appropriately, astronomers designed a special symbol for Pluto that looked like the letters "p" and "l" put together.

♇

When the other Club members met Pluto they were
extremely confused. He didn't fit into any familiar
categories such as gas giants or rocky planets.
For one thing, although he was in the outer part
of the Solar System like the largest planets,
Pluto was tiny.

"How could he be so little?" Jupiter wondered, his
great red spot pulsating in deep thought. Glancing
at Uranus he said, "I thought that only the inner
planets were small."

"He doesn't seem to me like an outer planet either,"
Uranus replied, "He's more like a ball of ice and rock."

Neptune was perplexed by another aspect of Pluto.
She found it odd that while most of the time Pluto was
the farthest member of the Planet Club from the Sun,
during part of his orbit he would move closer to the Sun
than she was.

"Pluto, please make up your mind," said Neptune,
her azure-blue gases swirling in bafflement.
"Do you want to be the farthest planet or the second
farthest planet? Whatever you decide is fine.
Just tell me, so that I know what I am."

"It's complicated," said Pluto, grinning an icy smile.
"I pass through a plethora of places. 'Plethora' means many,
so I don't have to choose between nearer or farther."

Suddenly Neptune had
a frightening thought
and her gases turned
bluer than usual.
"What if you crrrasshh into me?"
she said with a shiver.

Pluto replied reassuring, "Don't worry,
the plane of my orbit is tilted compared to yours.
Like two space coaster cars on loops that are
slanted at different angles, we won't
slam into each other."

When astronomers eventually discovered that Pluto
has many moons, Mars was upset. His rusty color
reddened as he complained to Mercury.

"For a pipsqueak planet how did Pluto end up
with more moons than me?" Mars grumbled.
"He seems to have twice as many, in fact."

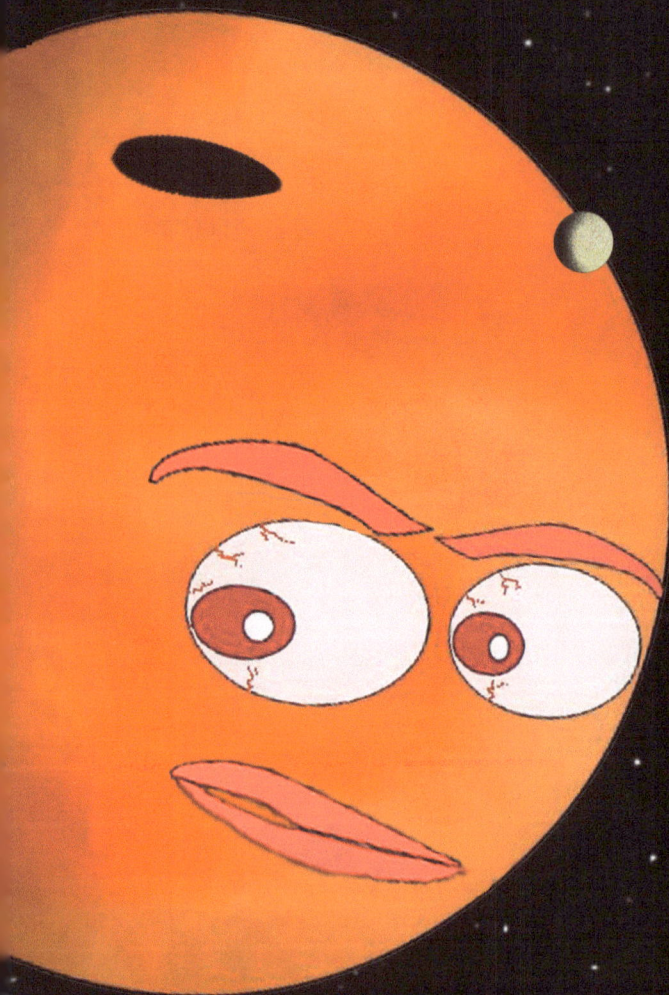

"Well I don't have any," said Mercury.
"A petite planet, if he has moons at all,
should have one or two at the most. It just
doesn't seem normal to have more than that.
Pluto certainly dances to his own tune."

Astronomers mapped out the orbits of
Pluto's moons very carefully, particularly
that of its largest moon Charon.
They figured out how much mass Pluto
must have to cause the gravitational
tugs that produce such motions.

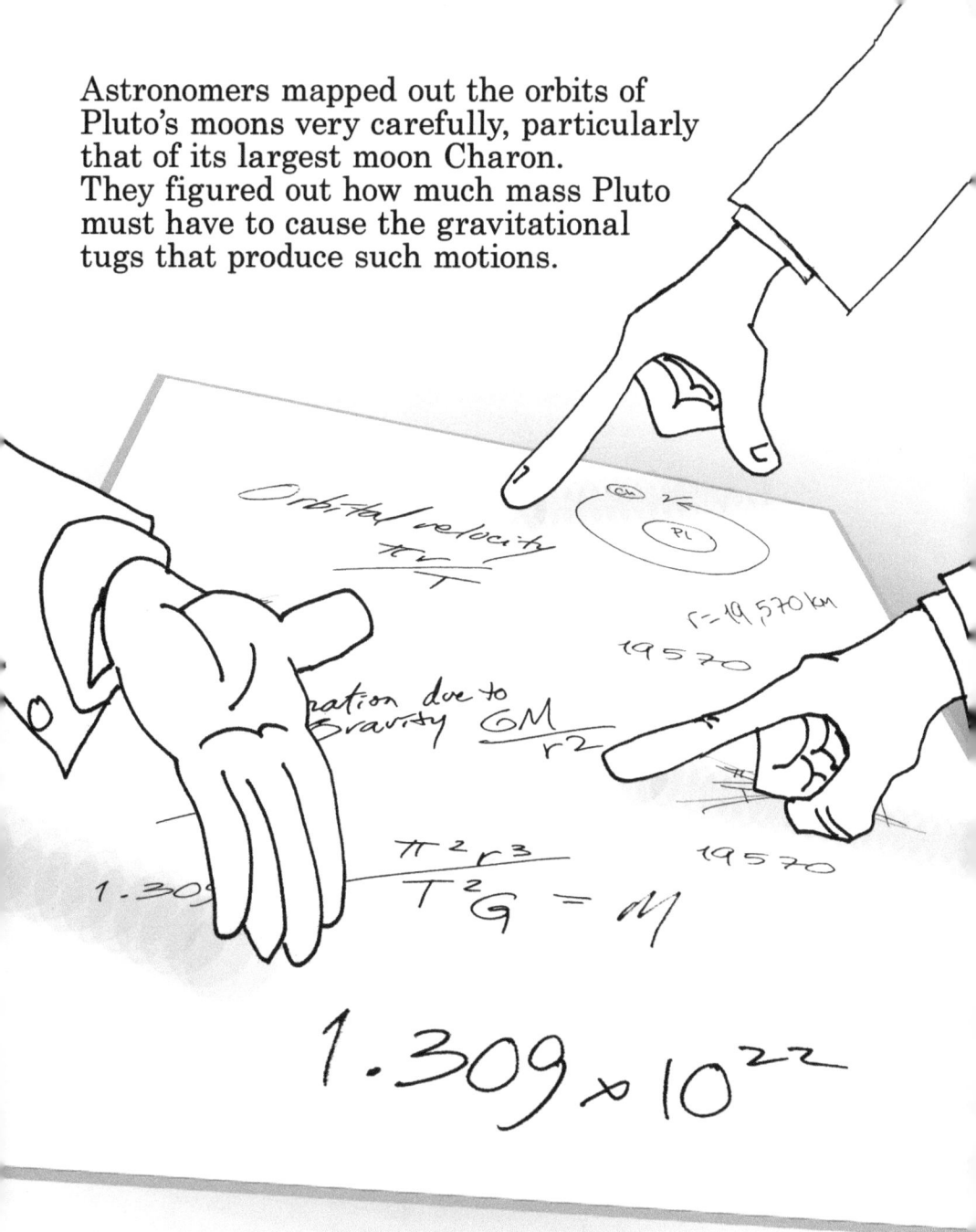

This method offered astronomers a way of "weighing"
Pluto. Pluto turned out to weigh about 400 times
lighter than Earth and even less than many moons
circling other planets in the Solar System!

"Let me get this straight," said Jupiter to Saturn.
"Pluto is lighter than some of our own moons
and is still a planet. How could that be?"

Saturn twirled her rings
as she listened intently.
"He's round like us," she replied.
"But in many ways he is different."

Pluto started to feel a bit like a platypus,
a creature that, with its duckbill, fur, and pouch,
didn't fit into any categories.

"They should have named me 'Plutopus,'" he said
to Venus. "I'm just a jumble of things
that don't match."

Venus
was not very
sympathetic. "Well, at
least you don't have to carry
around a thick hot atmosphere,"
she replied while adjusting her
heavy layers. "I would enjoy some
chilly weather every once in a while."

To make matters worse, Pluto learned that
many astronomers were debating whether or
not he qualified at all for being a planet.
One day in 2006, he received the bad news:
The International Astronomical Union, the
leading group of astronomers, had voted to
kick him out of the Planet Club.

Earth tried hard to cheer up Pluto.
"Those silly astronomers," she said.
"They keep changing their minds about
things. For a long time they thought
that all the other planets revolved around me.
They didn't even let me into the Club until
they discovered that I revolve around
the Sun like the others. Maybe they'll
change their minds again and let you
back into the Club."

Pluto wasn't very optimistic, especially after
he found out the main reason he was dismissed
from the Planet Club.

He learned about another round object that was
heavier than him, orbited the Sun, and yet wasn't
a club member. The new body, called Eris, lived
in an icy place called the Kuiper belt, where many
comets began their journeys.

After a team of astronomers led by Mike Brown discovered Eris, the International Astronomical Union recognized that there could be many objects in the Kuiper belt that were heavier than Pluto. The organization realized that they needed to make a choice—either to enlarge greatly the membership size of the Planet Club or to tighten its rules so that objects like Pluto that are too weak to "clear the neighborhoods around their orbits" would be excluded.

Planets "clearing their neighborhoods" meant collecting, through their gravitational pull, all other massive objects that lie within their part of space.

It is like a strong bar magnet picking up all the paper clips in a bowl. Pluto could not do so and therefore did not meet that standard.

The International Astronomical Union held a long, heated debate. Finally, its members voted to create two categories: planets and dwarf planets. Planets are round, orbit the Sun, don't orbit anything else, and clear their neighborhoods.

The first eight members of the Planet Club met that definition. Dwarf planets met all the other rules, but didn't clear their neighborhoods. Pluto was moved to that category, which also included Eris and the largest asteroid Ceres.

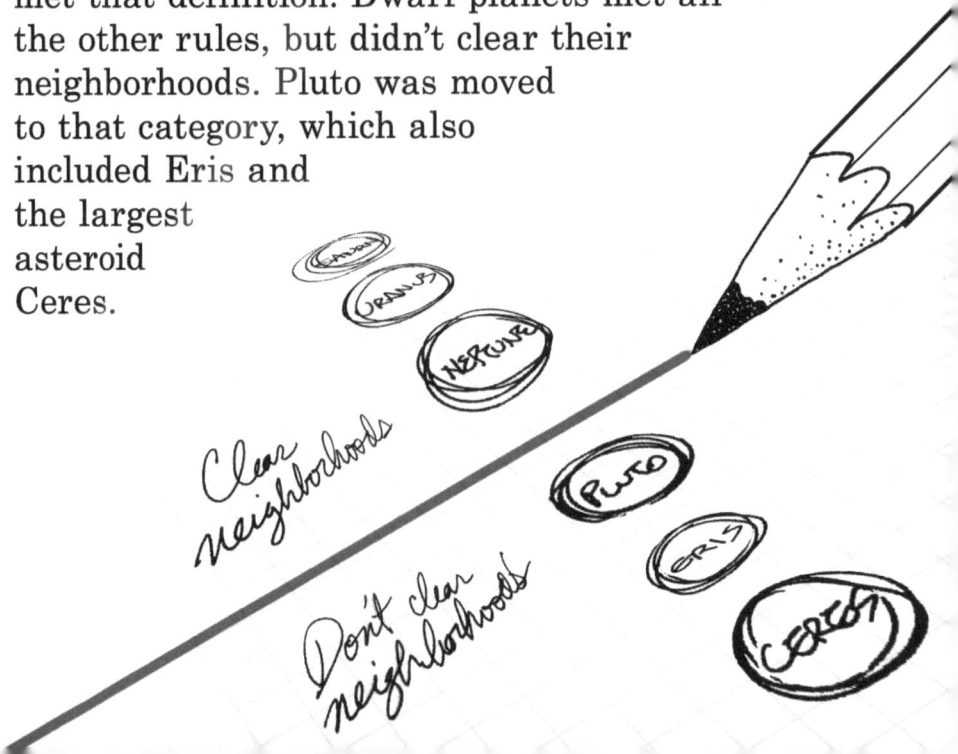

Clear neighborhoods

Don't clear neighborhoods

After his demotion, Pluto went through some sad times.
Earth tried to divert him by asking him about words
starting with "pl," but he couldn't concentrate enough
to think of any new ones.

Instead, Pluto kept thinking
of "dw" words such as
"dwindling"
and "dweeb."

What, he wondered, does it mean
to be a dwarf planet anyway?

Though mad at Eris for creating the problem,
Pluto decided to try and get to know him.
Much to his surprise, he and Eris had a lot
in common.

Eris's jacket of frozen chemicals matched his outer
layers too—with a somewhat different mixture of ices.
While Eris was heavier, they were both around the
same size in terms of radius.

Eris was very friendly too!

It was a shame, Pluto thought, that they both
couldn't be in the Planet Club together.

Finally in 2008, Earth brought Pluto some
exciting news. "The International Astronomical
Union has voted to form a new club," said Earth.
"The membership is open to all dwarf planets
beyond Neptune's orbit. I'm happy to report that
you have been admitted."

"That's nice," said Pluto.

"You and Eris are both
members, in fact,"
remarked Earth.

"What's the club's name?" asked Pluto.

"It is called the Plutoids—named after you! Surprise!" Earth gleefully replied.

Pluto was so excited! He couldn't wait to tell his new friend Eris.

"Hey Eris!" he shouted. "Guess what?
Now you are in my club, The Plutoids.
I expect that soon we'll have plenty of
new members! Maybe even a plethora!
We're going to have so much fun
playing together!"

It was a proud day for Pluto indeed!

www.ingramcontent.com/pod-product-compliance
Lightning Source LLC
Chambersburg PA
CBHW040346060426
42445CB00029B/17

* 9 780615 855110 *